A Guide for Using

Number the Stars

in the Classroom

Based on the novel written by Lois Lowry

This guide written by **Kathy Jordan**

Illustrated by **Sue Fullam and Keith Vasconcelles**

Teacher Created Resources, Inc.
6421 Industry Way
Westminster, CA 92683
www.teachercreated.com

ISBN: 978-1-55734-424-3

©1993 Teacher Created Resources, Inc.
Reprinted, 2007
Made in U.S.A.

Table of Contents

Introduction

A good book can touch our lives like a good friend. Within its pages are words and characters that can inspire us to achieve our highest ideals. We can turn to it for companionship, recreation, comfort, and guidance. It also gives us a cherished story to hold in our hearts forever.

In *Literature Units,* great care has been taken to select books that are sure to become good friends!

Teachers who use this literature unit will find the following features to supplement their own valuable ideas.

- Sample Lesson Plans

- Pre-reading Activities

- A Biographical Sketch and Picture of the Author

- A Book Summary

- Vocabulary Lists and Suggested Vocabulary Activities

- Chapters grouped for study, with each section including:

    – *quizzes*

    – *hands-on projects*

    – *cooperative learning activities*

    – *cross-curriculum connections*

    – *extensions into the reader's own life*

- Post-reading Activities

- Book Report Ideas

- Research Ideas

- A Culminating Activity

- Three Unit Test Options

- A Bibliography

- An Answer Key

We are confident that this unit will be a valuable addition to your planning, and hope that, as you use our ideas, your students will increase the circle of "friends" that they have in books!

Sample Lesson Plan

Each of the lessons suggested below can take from one to several days to complete.

LESSON 1

- Introduce and complete some or all of the pre-reading activities.
- Read "About the Author" with your students. (page 6)
- Introduce the section 1 vocabulary list. (page 8)

LESSON 2

- Read chapters 1-4. As you read, place the vocabulary words in the context of the story and discuss their meanings.
- Choose a vocabulary activity. (page 9)
- Have students compare and contrast characters. (page 11)
- Discuss the elements of fiction, and have students work in small groups to complete the activity. (page 12)
- Discuss the book in terms of geography. (page 13)
- Begin Reading Response Journals. (page 14)
- Administer the section 1 quiz. (page 10)
- Introduce the section 2 vocabulary list. (page 8)

LESSON 3

- Read Chapters 5-8.
- Choose a vocabulary activity. (page 9)
- Make a Danish raspberry dessert. (page 16)
- Do a Quick Write—Quick Share. (page 17)
- Have students write poetry relating to the book. (page 18)
- Write a postcard to Papa. (page 19)
- Administer the section 2 quiz. (page 8)
- Introduce the section 3 vocabulary list. (page 8)

LESSON 4

- Read chapters 9-12.
- Choose a vocabulary activity. (page 9)
- Perform reader's theater. (page 21)
- Research in groups the rescue of Danish Jews. (pages 22 and 23)
- Make invisible ink and send messages. (page 24)
- Have students complete the survey on page 25.
- Administer the section 3 quiz.
- Introduce the section 4 vocabulary list. (page 8)

LESSON 5

- Read chapters 13-15.
- Choose a vocabulary activity. (page 9)
- Make murals. (page 27)
- Have students work in small groups to prepare writing activities on the topic of peace. (page 28)
- Discuss the book in terms of math. (page 29)
- Find ways to make new friends with the activity on page 30. (You may want to begin this right after reading the chapters, since it takes one full week.)
- Administer the section 4 quiz. (page 26)
- Introduce the section 5 vocabulary list. (page 8)

LESSON 6

- Read chapters 16-Afterword.
- Choose a vocabulary activity. (page 9)
- Have students begin work on the Star of David Story Web. (page 33)
- Work in small groups to complete the Meet the Characters activity. (page 34)
- Discuss the book in terms of art. (page 35)
- Simulate the escape scene. (page 36)
- Administer the section 5 quiz. (page 32)

LESSON 7

- Discuss any questions your students may have about the story. (page 37)
- Assign book reports and research projects. (pages 38 and 39)
- Begin work on the culminating activity. (pages 40-42)

LESSON 8

- Administer Unit Tests 1, 2, and/or 3. (pages 43-45)
- Discuss the test answers and responses.
- Discuss the students' opinions and enjoyment of the book.
- Provide a list of related reading for the students. (page 46)

LESSON 9

- Complete the culminating activity (pages 43-45). Have the reunion of the two families, with the "news media" there to record the human interest story.

4

Before the Book

Before the students begin reading *Number the Stars*, do some pre-reading activities to stimulate their interest in the book.

1. Predict what the book might be about by looking at the cover.

2. Think about the title of the book, and predict what it might be about.

3. Ask the children if they are familiar with Lois Lowry. See if they have read any of her other books.

4. Ask the students what they know about World War II.

5. Have the students look up the Nazis in a reference book and discuss what their goals were in World War II.

6. Ask the children to work in small groups, or individually, to define the word "freedom."

7. Ask the students what a symbol is. Lead them into a discussion of the many symbols we use today (e.g., the flag, a hood ornament on a car, a cross, clothing logos, etc.). Have students make a collage depicting as many symbols as they can think of.

8. Discuss historical fiction. Have the students write short stories, based on an actual account from history, especially from World War II.

9. Ask students to think about the following questions and decide how they would respond to each of them.

   Have you ever:

   – wondered what it would be like to live somewhere else?

   – traveled to another country?

   – had to keep a secret?

   – been very afraid?

   – been called upon to be very brave?

About the Author

A group of teachers and librarians were listening to Lois Lowry speak when one of them asked her why she wrote books for adolescents. Her reply was that she hoped to make the reader feel "less alone." Those are simple words, and yet profound. Today, perhaps more than ever, adolescents need a sense of belonging, of fitting in, of having a purpose in life. To quote Lois Lowry:

> *Adolescence is very often a painfully lonely time; and it is a time when communication is difficult. A book can be a vehicle for communication; and a book can alleviate the sense of isolation that sometimes makes growing up lonely. Walking through a scary place is easier if you know that someone else has walked there once, and survived.*

Students who read *Number the Stars* are sure to identify with the emotions felt by the characters, even though the origins are different.

Lois Lowry was born on March 20, 1937, in Honolulu, Hawaii. Her father, Robert E. Hammbersberg, was a dentist, and her mother's name was Katherine. Lois attended Brown University from 1954 to 1956, and received her Bachelor of Arts degree from the University of Maine in 1972. In 1956 she married Donald Grey Lowry. They had four children named Alix, Grey, Kristin, and Benjamin.

Lois Lowry says that she can still remember the feeling of excitement that she had when she first discovered, at about four years of age, that sounds made words, words made sentences, and sentences made stories. She decided right then to become a writer, and held onto that dream throughout her life. When she graduated from high school in 1954, her high school yearbook described her as a "future novelist."

However, she didn't begin to write immediately. She had a family to care for, her education to complete and more of life to experience. When she began to write, she sometimes drew on her own experiences, sometimes used experiences of a friend (as she did in *Number the Stars*), and sometimes just used her wonderful imagination.

Lois received the Newbery Award for *Number the Stars* in 1990, and the International Reading Association award for children's literature in 1978 for *A Summer to Die*.

Today, Lois Lowry lives in an old house on Beacon Hill in Boston that has brick sidewalks and gaslights outside. Neighborhood rumors have it that Herman Melville (who wrote *Moby Dick*) once lived in that same house.

(Information about Lois Lowry was taken from *Something About the Author*, Gale Research, Volume 23.)

6

Number the Stars
by Lois Lowry
(Dell, 1989)

(Available in Canada from Doubleday Dell Seal, in the UK from Lions,
and in Australia from Transworld Publishers)

Annemarie Johansen and her best friend, Ellen Rosen, are racing home from school when they are stopped by German soldiers on the corner. The girls think this is just another inconvenience that they need to contend with since the occupation of Denmark by the Nazis. However, they do not realize that soldiers on street corners and rationed food are only the beginning of their trials.

Since Annemarie and her family are Protestant they are safe, but Ellen's family is Jewish. When the Rosens get word that they are about to be relocated, they decide to find a way to escape. The Johansens agree to allow Ellen to live with them temporarily, and the girls embark on an adventure designed to save Ellen's life.

Mrs. Johansen's brother, Henrik, owns a fishing boat, which he normally uses to earn his living. During the Nazi occupation, he also uses it to help smuggle Jews out of Denmark into Sweden. However, he finds that his efforts are being thwarted by German soldiers who realize that Jews are escaping, and begin to suspect the local fishermen.

Annemarie discovers that once the Rosens are aboard the fishing boat, her Uncle Henrik is missing a secret packet that he needs in order to make the journey successful. In spite of her fear, Annemarie knows that she must deliver the packet. She is stopped by German soldiers while on her way to the boat and narrowly escapes with the packet hidden in Uncle Henrik's lunch.

The mysterious item hidden in the packet, and the historical relevance of it are not revealed until the very end of the book. Annemarie discovers that she has played a major part in saving Ellen's life, and that bravery is thinking about what needs to be done, not about how frightened she is.

Vocabulary Lists

On this page are vocabulary lists which correspond to each sectional grouping of chapters.
Vocabulary activity ideas can be found on page 9 of this book.

SECTION 1
(Chapters 1 - 4)

lanky	*Halte*
Nazi	occupation
sabotage	rationed
kroner	swastika
disdainfully	synagogue
rabbi	submerged

SECTION 2
(Chapters 5 - 8)

Star of David	pose
tentatively	exasperation
shoreline	hazy
relocate	military arrest
specter	imprinted

SECTION 3
(Chapters 9 - 12)

rhythmically	mourning
urgency	staccato
typhus	Godspeed
pride	exhausted
unfamiliar	surge

SECTION 4
(Chapters 13 - 15)

drunkard	sprawling
stricken	donned
latticed	visible
exasperated	saliva
contempt	tantalize

SECTION 5
(Chapters 16 - 17)

warily	concealed
courageous	anthem
balcony	executed
deprivation	heroine
permeated	cocaine

8

Vocabulary Activity Ideas

You can help your students learn and retain the vocabulary in *Number the Stars* by providing them with interesting vocabulary activities. Here are some ideas to try.

❏ People of all ages like to make and solve puzzles. Ask your students to make their own **Crossword Puzzles** or **Wordsearch Puzzles** using the vocabulary words from the story.

❏ Challenge your students to a **Vocabulary Bee!** This is similar to a spelling bee, but in addition to spelling each word correctly, the game participants must correctly define the words as well.

❏ Play **Vocabulary Concentration.** The goal of this game is to match vocabulary words with their definitions. Divide the class into groups of two to five students. Have students make two sets of the cards the same size and color. On one set have them write the vocabulary words. On the second set have them write the definitions. All cards are mixed together and placed face down on a table. A player picks two cards. If the cards match (the word with its definitions) the player keeps the pair of cards and takes another turn. If the cards do not match, they are returned to their places face down on the table, and another player takes a turn. Players must concentrate to remember the location of the words and their definitions. The game continues until all matches have been made. This is an ideal activity for free exploration time.

❏ Students will enjoy playing **Vocabulary Basketball** as a means of reviewing the spelling and definition of each word. Small groups of students will compete as a team against another small group. A reader from one team will select a vocabulary word which he or she will call out to the other team. The student who is up will spell and define the word. If that student is correct, he/she will be given a chance to throw a bean bag into a wastebasket for 3 points. (Spelling and definition each count as one point, and the throw is worth one point.) If the information given is incorrect, the question will go to the other team.

❏ A new twist to an old idea is to have students make **Vocabulary Flashcards** in the shape of one of the symbols used in *Number the Stars* (e.g., the Star of David, a Danish flag, King Christian X's crown, etc.). Flashcards can be used for vocabulary review games created for or by the class.

❏ Ask your students to create paragraphs which use the vocabulary words to present **History Lessons** that relate to the time period of the novel.

❏ Challenge your students to use a specific vocabulary word from the story at least **10 Times in One Day.** They must keep a record of when, how, and why the word was used.

❏ As a group activity, have students work together to create an **Illustrated Dictionary** of the vocabulary words.

❏ Play **Vocabulary Charades.** In this game, vocabulary words are acted out!

You probably have many more ideas to add to this list. Try them! See if experiencing vocabulary on a personal level increases your students' vocabulary interest and retention.

Quiz Time!

1. On the back of this paper, write a one paragraph summary of the major events that happened in these four chapters.

2. Describe what happens to Annemarie, Ellen, and Kirsti on their way home from school.

   _____

   _____

3. What is "De Frie Danske"? Who brought it and why? _____

   _____

   _____

4. Who are the Resistance fighters?_____

   _____

   _____

5. Who is Lise and what happened to her? _____

   _____

   _____

6. On the back of this page, list three ways in which the Nazi occupation changed the lives of the citizens of Copenhagen.

7. What religion do the Rosens practice? Why is that a problem? _____

   _____

8. What is wrong with Kirsti's new shoes? How is this problem solved? _____

   _____

9. Why does Ellen spend the night with Annemarie? _____

   _____

10. The following statements are events that have happened in Chapters 1 and 2. Put a 1 next to the event that happened first, a 2 next to the event that happened next, and so on until all 6 events are numbered in the order in which they occurred.

    _____ Kirsti asked Mama for cupcakes.

    _____ Annemarie thought about King Christian X.

    _____ Annemarie, Ellen, and Kirsti raced home from school.

    _____ Annemarie thought about Lise, and what happened to her.

    _____ The girls were stopped by the German soldiers.

    _____ Annemarie told Kirsti a fairy tale.

Compare and Contrast

One of the ways we develop a better understanding of the characters in a story is by comparing and contrasting them. Under the name of each character, write several phrases to describe that person, using his/her physical characteristics and personality traits.

Annemarie
_____
_____
_____
_____
_____
_____

Ellen
_____
_____
_____
_____
_____
_____

Kirsti
_____
_____
_____
_____
_____
_____

The Giraffe
_____
_____
_____
_____
_____
_____

Now, select two of the characters and draw pictures of them. Underneath your illustrations write a paragraph about each of them. Use your descriptive phrases to guide your writing. Include ways in which the characters are *alike* and how they are *different*.

Elements of Fiction

Is *Number the Stars* a fiction or nonfiction story? Meet in a small group to decide. Read or tell the familiar story of Little Red Riding Hood. As a group, discuss the elements that make this a fictional story. Then discuss these elements of fiction as they apply to *Number the Stars*.

As a group, create a poster or chart for the class showing the elements of fiction found in *Number the Stars*. Use the *Little Red Riding Hood* sample below to guide you with your project. Find creative ways to display your ideas. For instance, you might put each element of fiction on a building block and write the answer in the center of the block. Any item with parts, such as a picket fence or a Christmas tree with ornaments will work.

Elements of Fiction Sample

Element	Definition	Red Riding Hood
Setting	Time Place	Once upon a time In the woods
Theme	Story meaning	Obedience to parents
Protagonist	Main character	Red Riding Hood
Antagonist	Creates conflict for main character	Bad Wolf
Plot	What the story is about	A girl disobeys her mother and takes a shortcut through the woods. She meets a wolf who tricks her by disguising himself as her grandmother. They are saved by a friendly woodsman.
Point of View	Who is telling the story	Third person

Note:

A story written in the *first* person is one in which the author uses the words "I" and "me" when telling the story (e.g., I watched the boat sail away.).

When the author directs the story to you, he or she is using the *second* person. He may say, "You will see the boat sail away."

A story written in the *third* person refers to the author's use of the words "he," "she," or "they" in the story (e.g., She sailed the boat.).

Where in the World Are We?

Use an atlas to help you label the following countries and their capitals on the map below. Then use the chart to color them as follows:

Country	*Color*	*Occupied?*
Denmark	red	_____
Sweden	yellow	_____
Norway	blue	_____
Finland	green	_____
Poland	purple	_____
Germany	brown	_____

Now, research each country in an encyclopedia to find out whether or not they were occupied by Germany during World War II. Fill in the chart above by writing "Yes" or "No" on the lines.

Reading Response Journals

One reason avid readers are drawn to literature is what it does for them on a personal level. They are intrigued with how it triggers their imaginations, what it makes them ponder, and how it makes them see and shape themselves. To assist your students in experiencing this for themselves, incorporate Reading Response Journals in your plans. In these journals, students can be encouraged to respond to the story in a number of ways. Here are a few ideas.

- Tell the students that the purpose of the journal is to record their thoughts, ideas, observations, and questions as they read a book.

- Provide students with, or ask them to suggest, topics from the story that may stimulate writing. Here are two examples from the chapters in Section 1.

    1. Annemarie has found that her home and country have been changed because of the occupation of the Nazis. How would you feel if this happened to you? How would your life today be changed if a foreign power took over?

    2. Annemarie's best friend, Ellen, was Jewish. Have you ever had a friend that had a different religion or nationality? How were you alike? How were you different?

- After the reading of each chapter, encourage students to write one or more new things they learned.

- Ask students to draw their responses to certain events or characters in the story.

- Suggest to your students that they write "diary-type" responses to their reading by selecting a character and describing events from the character's point of view.

- Encourage students to bring their journal ideas to life by using them to create plays, stories, songs, art displays, and debates.

- Give students quotes from the novel and ask them to write their own responses. Make sure to do this before you discuss the quotations in class. In groups, they could list the different ways students can respond to the same quote.

Allow students time to write in their journals daily. To evaluate the journals, you may wish to use the following guidelines.

- Personal reflections will be read by the teacher, but no corrections or letter grades will be assigned. Credit is given for effort, and all students who sincerely try will be awarded credit. If a grade is desired for this type of entry, grade according to the number of journal entries completed. For example, if five journal assignments were made and the students conscientiously completes all five, then he or she should receive an "A."

- Nonjudgmental teacher responses should be made as you read the journals to let the students know that you are reading and enjoying their journals.

Quiz Time!

1. Describe what happens in the middle of the night when Ellen stays with Annemarie.

   _____

   _____

2. What makes the German soldiers suspicious of Ellen's identity?_____

   _____

   _____

3. What does Papa do to answer the German soldier's questions about Ellen? _____

   _____

   _____

4. Describe how the German soldiers treat the family. _____

   _____

   _____

5. What does the code word "cigarettes" mean?_____

   _____

   _____

6. What is Annemarie afraid that Kirsti will do on the train ride to visit Uncle Henrik?_____

   _____

   _____

7. Describe Uncle Henrik's house and the surrounding land._____

   _____

   _____

8. What does Ellen say that her mother is afraid of? _____

   _____

   _____

9. What does Uncle Henrik say happened to Great-aunt Birte? _____

   _____

   _____

10. On the back of this page, write a paragraph describing Uncle Henrik's housekeeping, and Mama's reaction to it.

What's for Dessert?

Annemarie and her family brought Ellen to Uncle Henrik's house in the country. Since Uncle Henrik owned a cow, butter and cream were available. What wonderful things they could make, especially if they could find a few wild raspberries! They might not be able to make frosted cupcakes that Kirsti longed for, but if they could find a little sugar and cinnamon, they could prepare a favorite Danish recipe—Arme Riddere (which translates to "Poor Knight").

Poor Knight's Dessert

Ingredients:

1 box frozen raspberries   6 tablespoons (90 mL) sugar

(strawberries may be substituted)   1½ teaspoons (8 mL) cinnamon

8 slices white bread   1 stick (¼ pound/112 g) butter

1 cup (250 mL) milk

Raspberry Sauce:

Put raspberries in a blender or mash by hand. Squeeze through a sieve to remove seeds. Warm just before serving.

Bread:

Dry 8 slices of bread by baking at 150° Fahrenheit (65° Celsius) for 15 minutes on each side, or until dry but not brown. Spoon 2 tablespoons (30 mL) of milk over each slice of bread. Sprinkle the bread slices evenly with the sugar and cinnamon. Melt half of the butter in a large skillet. Fry the bread in the butter, starting with the unsugared side, and turning when nicely browned. Use the remaining butter to continue frying the bread.

Serve with warm raspberry sauce. Makes 4 servings of 2 slices each.

Quick Write—Quick Share

Write the following topic ideas on the board, or make copies of this page for the students. Have students select a topic and begin writing about it, nonstop, for 10 or 15 minutes. They may either use complete sentences or phrases. The purpose of this activity is for students to get ideas down on paper and develop fluency in writing. It should not be graded.

Topic 1

Ellen has had some practice acting in school, but now she is called upon to "perform" in order to save her life. She must be very brave. Write about a time when you had to be brave. Did you have to act like everything was fine to protect someone or yourself? How did you feel?

Topic 2

Annemarie and Ellen are best friends and share many secrets while they are spending the night together. Write about your best friend. Do you ever spend the night together? What do you enjoy talking about? What qualities does your friend have?

Topic 3

These chapters tell about a time when people are very frightened. Write about a time when you were afraid. What happened? Who was there? Would you feel differently if faced with the same situation today?

Topic 4

This story takes place in Denmark during World War II, when it is occupied by Germany. What do you think it would be like to live under these circumstances? What could you do, or not do? What things would you not have? How would you feel?

After the students have done their free-writing, organize them into groups according to the topics they have chosen. Ask the students to share their writing with the group. Together each group can make a collage on a sheet of poster board to illustrate that topic. The title of the collages can be as follows:

Topic 1 - Bravery   **Topic 3** - Fear

Topic 2 - Friendship   **Topic 4** - Occupied

Of course, students may have original, creative titles of their own to suggest and should be encouraged to use them.

Poetry Possibilities

The characters and action in *Number the Stars* can be used to create poetry. Try writing one of the following types of poems using the story or characters as a topic.

Diamante

The idea of a diamante is to go from one subject (line 1) to another subject (sometimes opposite of line 1) at the bottom of the poem (line 7).

> Line 1- one noun (subject #1)
>
> Line 2 - two adjectives describing subject #1
>
> Line 3 - three participles, ending in "ing", telling about subject #1
>
> Line 4 - four nouns (first 2 relating to subject #1, and the second 2 relating to subject #2)
>
> Line 5 - three participles, telling about subject #2
>
> Line 6 - two adjectives describing subject #2
>
> Line 7 - one noun (subject #2)

Here is an example:

Mama
neat, clean
scrubbing, working, helping
wife, mother, farmer, sailor
seafaring, fishing, leaving
rough, sloppy
Uncle Henrik

Part of Speech Poem

Using the basic parts of speech, construct a poem as follows:

> Line 1 - a noun
>
> Line 2 - one or two adjectives, describing that noun
>
> Line 3 - a verb phrase
>
> Line 4 - one or two adverbs relating to the verb
>
> Line 5 - proper noun referring to line 1

Here is an example:

Sister
young, innocent
chases the kitten
quickly, noisily
Kirsti

A Postcard to Papa

In the space below, design a postcard to send to Papa in Copenhagen. Using the descriptions in the book, draw the countryside, the farm of Uncle Henrik, the seashore, or a fishing boat.

In the box below, write a message to Papa telling him of the trip to Uncle Henrik's. Remember that the Nazis might intercept the mail, so you will need to write anything about Ellen in code. Cut out the postcard and the message. Glue the message to the back of the postcard. Share the postcard with the class.

Quiz Time!

1. Why does Mama lie to Annemarie? _____

   _____

   _____

2. What is the surprise Ellen receives during the funeral of Great-aunt Birte? Describe Ellen's
   reaction to the surprise.

   _____

   _____

3. How does Mama keep the soldiers from opening the casket? _____

   _____

   _____

4. What is the meaning of the Psalm read at the funeral? _____

   _____

   _____

5. What is in the casket? _____

   _____

6. What does Peter give to the baby? Why? _____

   _____

   _____

7. Peter gives Mr. Rosen a paper-wrapped package. What instructions does Peter give to Mr. Rosen?

   _____

   _____

8. Describe the plan that Peter devises to get the group safely away. _____

   _____

   _____

9. How long is Mama supposed to be gone? How long is she actually gone? _____

   _____

   _____

10. What do you think has happened to Mama? _____

    _____

    _____

Reader's Theater

Reader's Theater is an exciting and relatively easy method of providing students with the opportunity to perform a mini-play without the hassle of props, sets, elaborate costumes, or memorization. Students read the dialogue of a character in a book or become the narrators to provide background information and read the connecting words. The dialogue and narration may be read verbatim as the author has written it, or an elaboration may be written by the performing students.

Allow students to use pages from Chapter 10 to conduct a Reader's Theater. Have students highlight their parts and act out any movements. The narration and action should be minimized, with the emphasis placed on the dialogue. Meaning should be conveyed by voice, posture, and facial expression. Readers should keep their scripts with them. Position performers behind music stands or desks, if the narrative allows. Sometimes, performers dress in black so even their dress does not distract from their verbal performance.

Consider having students who play a musical instrument play appropriate music in the background to lend feeling and drama to the performance, similar to radio broadcasts of the past. Lacking that, sound tracks from classical music can often provide background music. For example, choose selections that convey the feeling of the staccato of the marching soldiers, the importance of the words of scripture, and the mystery in opening casket.

You may wish to have groups of students dramatize various passages from *Number the Stars* and present their Reader's Theater productions to another class, at an assembly, or to parents.

The Miracle Rescue

On April 9, 1940, Germany invaded the Scandinavian country of Denmark. King Christian X, the ruler of Denmark, knew his small country was no match for Hitler's forces. He surrendered after only a few hours of fighting. The Nazis decided to keep the Danish government in power as long as its officials met their demands. During the next three years of the German occupation, Danish Resistance Forces were formed and began to sabotage factories and transportation systems. As a result, the Nazis took over the government in August 1943.

In October 1943, Jewish people living in Denmark learned that the Nazis were planning to round up the entire Jewish population and send them to death camps. Within hours, over 7,000 Danish Jews were safely hidden in the homes of non-Jewish neighbors and friends. On the night of the Nazis' roundup, 284 Jews were arrested. The Nazis continued to search over the next month, and 200 more Danish Jews were located and sent to death camps.

Small groups of Jews, totaling approximately 7,200 people, were smuggled by Danish Resistance Fighters to fishing villages along the coast. From there, they were hidden in fishing boats in order to cross the 15-mile (9.3-kilometer) channel to Sweden, a neutral country. Many Resistance Fighters lost their lives taking part in this smuggling operation.

The Jews who were arrested by the Nazis were not forgotten. The Danish government persisted in knowing their whereabouts and even inspected the camps where they were being held. Nazi records indicate that 51 Danish Jews died in these camps from natural causes. The Danish authorities believe these deaths were the result of atrocious living conditions in the camps. There is no record of any Danish Jew being killed in a gas chamber by the Nazis.

After World War II when the Jews returned to their homes in Denmark, they found that their fellow countrymen had cared for and protected their property. Their homes were the same as when they had left to escape the Nazis.

The Danish people were certainly courageous and heroic. Their story provided a bright ray of hope during the dark days of World War II.

The Miracle Rescue *(cont.)*

For this activity, you will work in groups of two or three students. When you have completed the research, share your responses with the class.

1. The map below shows the European boundaries following World War I. Use the map to locate and color Denmark, Sweden, and Germany. Examine where Denmark is in relationship to Germany and Sweden. Locate Copenhagen, the capital of Denmark, which is the main setting in *Number the Stars*. How did Denmark's geographical location and features play a major role in the success of smuggling Danish Jews to Sweden?

2. Research to discover why Sweden remained neutral during World War II even though its neighboring countries had fallen victim to the Nazi war machine.

3. The Danish Resistance movement was primarily organized by very young men and women. If you had been a teenager living in Denmark in 1943, would you have been one of the Resistance Fighters? What qualities would you need in order to participate in this colossal operation at such a high risk?

4. How do you think the successful rescue of Danish Jews helped to spark Resistance efforts in other parts of German-occupied Europe?

5. Identify any current events or situations in the world today in which one group of people may be the target of oppression or injustice by its government. Are there any groups, similar to the Danish Resistance Fighters, who are striving to fight these injustices? Are these groups trying to fight this oppression using peaceful or violent tactics?

European Boundaries Following World War I

Secret Scientists

Peter gave Mr. Rosen a paper-wrapped packet and told him that it was very important that this be given to Uncle Henrik. What do you think was in it? Suppose you wanted to send a secret message to someone. Maybe you could invent an invisible ink and use it to send your message.

For this activity, you will work as a scientist would to invent an invisible ink. You will need to measure the ingredients very carefully and record the results in order to reproduce the ink.

Mix together some onion juice, lemon juice, and sugar. Measure and record the amounts carefully. Use your ink and a toothpick to write a message on a piece of paper. Allow the ink to dry. Hold the paper over a bright light bulb to see if your message is there.

Use the chart below to record your experiment. For each time the ink is made, record the formula (the quantities you used) and the results.

Hypothesis (What do you think will happen?) _____

_____

Experiment:

	Sugar	Onion Juice	Lemon Juice	Result
1.	_____	_____	_____	_____
2.	_____	_____	_____	_____
3.	_____	_____	_____	_____
4.	_____	_____	_____	_____
5.	_____	_____	_____	_____
6.	_____	_____	_____	_____

Conclusion (Which formula worked best?): _____

_____

_____

Note: Another common invisible ink can be made using equal parts of salt and hot water. Write your message on paper and allow it to dry completely. When rubbed with a pencil's lead, the message will magically appear! If time allows, compare both types of ink and decide which works better.

What Would You Do?

Put yourself in the Rosens' place. What would you do if you had to suddenly leave the country? What would you want to take with you? Remember that they could only take very small items that could be carried with them, such as a locket, a small picture, or perhaps a small book. What about your family? Would your parents choose something different from what you would consider valuable? Interview them to find out!

In the spaces below, list the names of each of your family members and find out what small things they would carry with them and what they would be most upset about leaving behind.

Name _____

Items to take _____

_____

_____

Hate to leave_____

_____

_____

Name _____

Items to take _____

_____

_____

Hate to leave_____

_____

_____

Name _____

Items to take _____

_____

_____

Hate to leave_____

_____

_____

Name _____

Items to take _____

_____

_____

Hate to leave_____

_____

_____

If you need more space, use the back of this page.

Quiz Time!

1. Describe what happens to Mama on the way back from the boat. _____

   _____

   _____

2. What does Annemarie find next to the house? _____

   _____

   _____

3. What instructions does Mama give Annemarie concerning the item she found next to the house?

   _____

   _____

4. What story does Annemarie think about on the path to the boat? _____

   _____

   _____

5. List the main characters in the story that Annemarie thought about. _____

   _____

   _____

6. How are the characters you named in question 5 like the ones in *Number the Stars*?

   _____

   _____

7. What are the instructions that Annemarie's mother gives her in case she is stopped?

   _____

   _____

8. On the back of this page, describe Annemarie's encounter with the German soldiers. Tell about their attitudes and actions, and Annemarie's reaction.

9. What does the German soldier find in the packet?_____

   _____

   _____

10. Using the back of this page, predict what you think will happen next. Tell where you think the Rosens are and what is in the packet. Remember, it's more important to be logical than absolutely correct.

Mood Murals

Think about the book, *Number the Stars*, and what has taken place so far. Mentally divide the novel into the four sections that have been read so far (i.e., Chapters 1-4, Chapters 5-8, Chapters 9-12, and Chapters 13-15).

What words would you use to describe the mood of each of these sections? A thesaurus or dictionary might give you some ideas. Divide a sheet of paper into 4 sections, and label each section with the chapter headings listed above. Next, put your "mood descriptions" under each heading. You may have been thinking about a particular scene when you chose those words, and if so, write down a few phrases to remind yourself why you made those word choices.

Next, think about the colors that remind you of those words. For instance, if you wrote down the word "stormy," you might think of the colors gray or black; but, if you wrote down the word "angry," perhaps the colors dark red, purple, or bright orange come to mind. Write these colors next to your descriptions.

Just a hint: Pastel or light colors are considered peaceful, happy colors. Dark or intense colors are often thought of as relating to intense emotions, such as anger and hatred. Blues and greens are considered cool colors, while reds and oranges are warm colors.

Now, take a piece of mural paper (butcher paper or bulletin board coverings work well) and divide it into 5 sections, one for each section you have read, and one for the last section. Draw a scene from each of the sections, as you listed on your paper, using the colors you felt would relate to the mood of that scene. Pastel chalks work well.

You may either predict what you think will happen at the end of the book, and draw that on your mural, or wait until the end of the book to fill the last section of your "Mood Mural."

Peace Begins With Us

Number the Stars takes place in the 1940's, when the world is torn by war. Annemarie Johansen and her best friend, Ellen Rosen, often reflect on a time when life was peaceful.

Think about the regions of the world today where war has become a way of life and where peace seems to be a distant dream. Meet with classmates in a small group and discuss ways of helping to achieve peace in the world. Then, work together on one of the writing projects below, or create a peace project of your own. Present your project to the class.

★ **Recipes for Peace.** Design a set of Recipes for Peace, listing ingredients and directions for attaining peace on large recipe cards or index cards for each recipe. Punch a hole in the top left corner of each card; strengthen the holes with reinforcers. Make a cover, compile the cards behind it, and slip a metal clasp ring through the holes.

★ **Peace Begins With Us.** Brainstorm with your group as many ways as you can think of to maintain peace among family members, school companions, or people in your community. Use a large piece of chart paper or poster board to write and illustrate the list. Display your chart in the classroom.

★ **I Get Angry When . . .** With the members of your group, brainstorm situations that cause students to become upset and angry. Try to come up with about five. Next, write the phrase "I Get Angry When . . ." on the top of each of five pieces of white construction paper. Complete the phrases with the situations that you brainstormed. Illustrate each. Display the papers in the classroom.

★ **I Used to Think That . . .** On a piece of paper, write the following sentence: I used to think that peace . . ., but now I know . . . . Discuss in your group the possible ways to complete the sentence. (For example, I used to think peace was none of my concern, but now I know I need to become involved.) Choose several sentence endings to use for this activity. Using sentence strip paper or strips of construction paper, write your completed sentences. Perhaps you could display these on a classroom bulletin board.

★ **Dear Abby.** Cut out "Dear Abby" or other advice column articles from the newspaper. Share them in your group. Then each of you should write your own questions about peace in a letter and address the letter to "Dear Abby" or another advice columnist. Your group becomes "Dear Abby." Exchange the letters among group members and write a response to each question. Share the letters and the responses with the rest of the class.

Calculator Connections

Use a calculator to solve the following problems. If your teacher agrees, you may want to work with a partner.

1. Shortly after World War II (in 1950) most of the people living in Denmark were people who had been born there. The population numbers are as follows: 4,200,960 were born in Denmark; 25,320 came from Germany; 18,280 came from Sweden; 7,890 came from Norway, and 3,790 came from the U.S.

   What was the total population of Denmark? _____

2. Using the figures above, what was the total of the foreign-born population? _____

3. What is the approximate percentage of people who were foreign-born? _____

   (**Hint:** Remember the rules for finding percents. Make a fraction of the numbers, then divide the numerator by the denominator. This will give you a decimal. Round it to the nearest hundredth. Convert that number to a percent by moving the decimal point two places to the right and adding a % sign.)

4. Now that you remember how to do percents, calculate the percentage of foreign-born people in Denmark in 1950 who came from:

   Sweden_____   Germany _____

   Norway_____   The United States _____

5. While religious freedom is guaranteed by the Danish constitution, 97% of the people are Lutheran. If the Danish population in 1950 was approximately 4,250,000, how many people were Lutheran?

   _____

6. The following statistics were made available in the 1950 census taken after World War II:

   518,600 people worked in agriculture

   721,000 people worked in industry, handicrafts, and construction

   316,000 people worked in commerce, banking, and service trades

   137,600 people worked in transportation and utilities

   210,000 people worked in professions, public administration, and education

   What was the total number of people discussed in this census?_____

   What percentage worked in agriculture? _____

Make New Friends

Annemarie's best friend Ellen has just left the country, and she probably won't return for a very long time, if ever. Have you ever had a good friend move away? Of course you can still write to your friend, but Annemarie won't be able to do that. When she gets back to Copenhagen, Annemarie will need to make new friends. That's not always easy, but it's worth the effort.

Try making a new friend this week! First, choose someone that you would like to get to know, or have the teacher assign you a partner. For the next week, the two of you will work together as partners on any class projects. Complete the following chart and use it as a guide to help the two of you get better acquainted.

Monday

You can't be someone's friend without getting to know them. Interview your partner to find out:

Name_____   Age_____

Address _____

Phone_____

Family members _____

_____

Hobbies _____

Now your partner can interview you!

Tuesday

Get better acquainted by asking your partner to complete these interview statements:

One thing I like about school is _____

One thing I dislike about school is _____

My dream is to someday_____

My favorite food is _____

My religion is _____

In my free time, I like to_____

My favorite TV show is _____

Make New Friends *(cont.)*

Wednesday

Work with one or two other sets of partners. Introduce your new friend to the group, and have him or her introduce you.

Thursday

Secretly do something nice for your new friend, such as give him or her a new pencil, or draw a picture of something he or she likes and leave it on his or her desk.

Friday

Pack a lunch for your friend! Now that you know him/her, pack a favorite sandwich and snack in a bag with his/her name on it. If your friend packs a lunch for you, too, you can have a Friendship Picnic at lunchtime.

After lunch, draw a Venn diagram on a large sheet of paper. Have one circle for yourself and one for your friend. Let the circles overlap in the middle, as shown below. Put the characteristics that both of you share in the middle where the circles overlap. Put the ways in which you are different in your own portion of the circle.

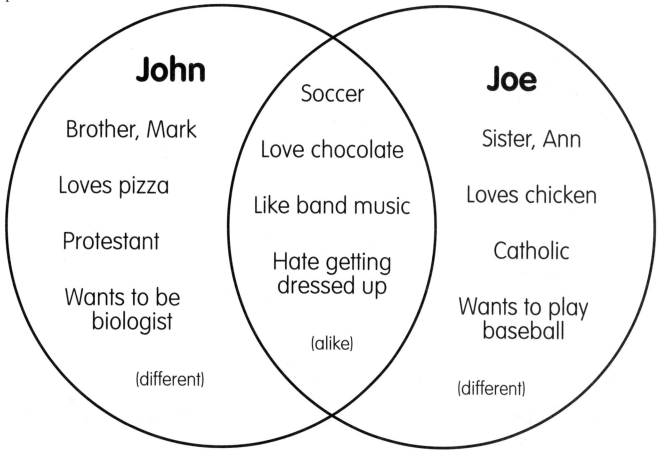

Quiz Time!

1. What is the first thing Annemarie had to try to do after returning to her uncle's house? _____

   _____

   _____

2. What is Uncle Henrik's definition of bravery? _____

   _____

   _____

3. Does Annemarie feel that she is brave? Why or why not? _____

   _____

   _____

4. How does Uncle Henrik get the Rosens to Sweden? _____

   _____

   _____

5. What does Annemarie learn about Peter? _____

   _____

   _____

6. What is the secret of the handkerchief?_____

   _____

   _____

7. Describe the city of Copenhagen when the war ended. _____

   _____

   _____

8. What does Annemarie finally learn about Lise's death? _____

   _____

   _____

9. Ellen's Star of David was kept in a safe place by Annemarie. Where has it been, and what will Annemarie do with it now?

   _____

   _____

10. On the back of this page, write one paragraph telling how much of this story is true, and how much is fiction. Be sure to include the characters, the war, the dogs, the handkerchief, and the king of Denmark.

Star of David Story Web

The Star of David has six points and is composed of two intersecting triangles. It is a symbol that has been used throughout the centuries to represent the Jews. For this activity, you will use the Star of David as the center for a story web to represent an overview of *Number the Stars*. Use the following information to make the star and to complete the web.

Choose a material such as plywood, cardboard, or straws to construct a pair of identical equilateral triangles. Paint these gold or cover them with foil. Overlap them to form a Star of David. Glue the triangles together. Mount the star on a piece of tag board, poster board, or plywood and place it in the center of your story web. (If regular glue won't hold, try using a glue gun which is available at craft stores. A glue gun can become very hot, so be sure an adult supervises this activity.)

In the center of the star, write the title of the story. At each of the six points, write one of the five W's and How of good reporting:

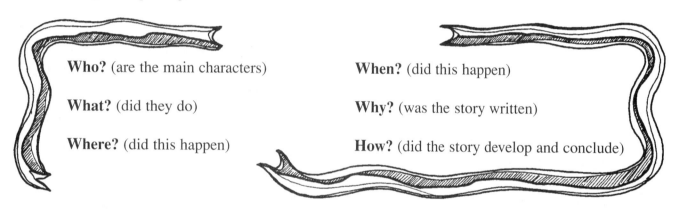

Who? (are the main characters)

What? (did they do)

Where? (did this happen)

When? (did this happen)

Why? (was the story written)

How? (did the story develop and conclude)

If you are working in groups, you may find that there is some disagreement about what the main idea of the story is, or why the story was written. That's okay. Write down your ideas, and try to come to a consensus on an idea about which you can all agree.

Once this information is recorded, see if you have space left to draw some characters, symbols, or scenes from the book. This project can then be used as a library display on Newbery Award books, or to advertise the book for another class.

Meet the Characters

Assign four or five students to a cooperative group. If you are doing the friendship activity in Section 4, you might put two of these pairs together to form a group. Have each student select one of the following characters: Annemarie, Ellen, Mama, Uncle Henrik, Peter Neilson, Lise.

Distribute copies of the character web below and have each student complete one for his or her character. Students may need to skim the previous chapters for information, but a few of the characters do not become "complete" until this last part of the book. After students have completed this part of the activity on their own, they will meet with their groups. They must stay in character during the rest of the activity, and speak in the first person (using "I" and "me"). Each character will introduce himself/herself to the group and tell the group what happened during the story from his/her point of view. Students must also include the web information. The group will then discuss and decide what the future will be for that person. If the character dies, then tell what would have happened if he or she had lived, or how the story might have changed because of that character's death.

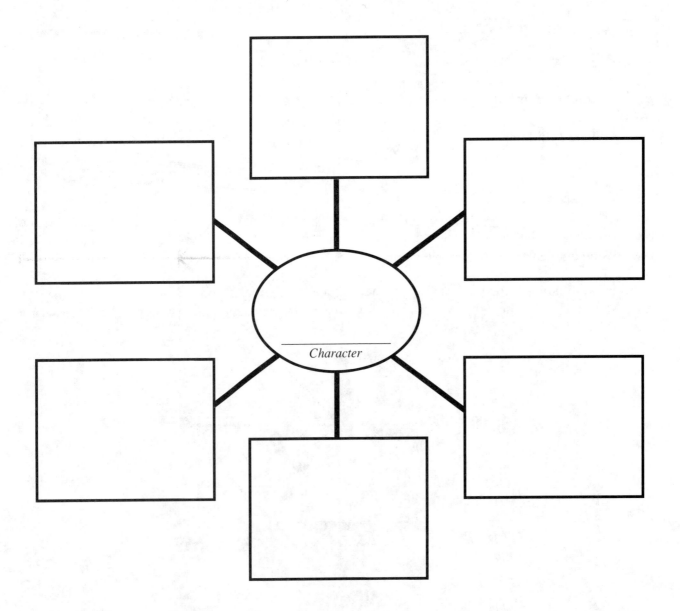

Character

Tessellations

The necklace that Annemarie saved for Ellen was a Star of David, which is a symbol used to represent the Jewish faith. The Star of David is made of two equilateral triangles (all of the sides are the same length). By placing one triangle over the other, a figure is formed that has 6 points, and each point forms a little triangle inside the figure.

Geometric shapes, such as triangles, have often been used to create wonderful patterns, like those used in mosaics. These are sometimes used to decorate chapels and other places of worship. These patterns are called tesselations.

Using an index card or a piece of tag board, make a template in the shape of a triangle. On a blank sheet of paper, try tracing around the template to create a pattern that is unique. The template can be arranged at any angle, and overlapped as many times as you like. You can create smaller triangles by intersecting one triangle with another. Use light and dark color patterns, or complementary colors to create very interesting effects. You will be amazed at what you can create using only one template for one shape!

Sample Tessellation

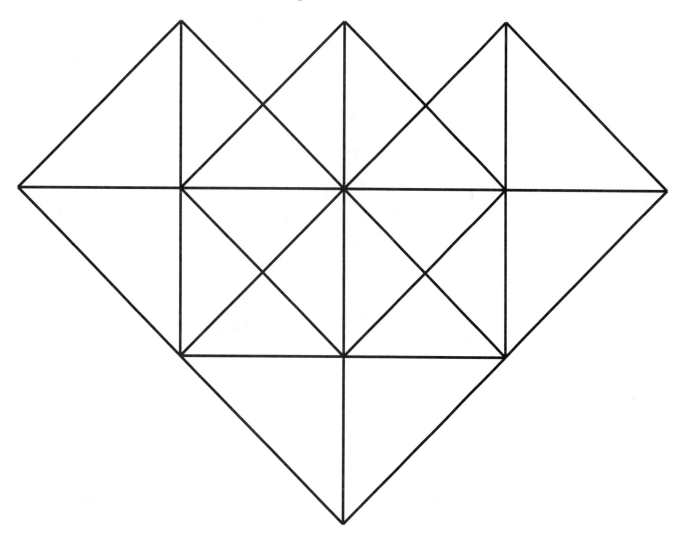

Simulation

Ellen and her family had to escape to Sweden in a dark, hidden compartment of the bottom of a ship. There were many people crammed into a very small space. What would that feel like? Sitting like that for a long time would be bad enough, but knowing that if you were caught you'd be killed, would add a great deal of tension to the trip. Could you do it? None of us knows what we can do until we are called upon to do it, but perhaps we can get a feel for what Ellen and her family went through.

Create a "secret compartment" in the bottom of a "boat" using a long table, some air mattresses, and a few large blankets.

Set the table in an open area of the classroom or school. Place the air mattresses underneath the table. The air mattresses should give the feeling of the boat's movement whenever one of the students moves. Put as many students as will fit under the table and place the blankets over the sides of the table to block out the light.

Students in the "secret compartment" must remain absolutely silent—no talking, no giggling, no moving—as the teacher creates the sound of footsteps on top of the table (simulating the German soldiers).

Some students will take this more seriously than others. If you really want to simulate the escape, try putting an open can of tuna fish inside the "boat," for the authentic odor; or splash a little water inside from a "leaky board." If students get silly, reinforce that this really happened to many people, and that their lives depended on being quiet and cooperative.

36

Any Questions?

When you finished reading *Number the Stars*, did you have some questions that were left unanswered? Write some of your questions here.

_____

_____

_____

Work in groups or by yourself to prepare possible answers for some or all of the questions you have asked above and those written below. When you have finished writing your predictions, share your ideas with the class.

- What happens to the Rosens in Sweden? Do they settle there, or move on to someplace else? Does Papa get a job teaching again in another country?

- Now that Annemarie knows the secret of the handkerchief, does she encounter German soldiers again and need to keep this information to herself?

- What is Denmark like after the war for the Johansens? How long does it take to begin to get things like coffee, sugar, and butter? Does Kirsti get her cupcakes?

- Do Annemarie and Ellen ever see each other again? If so, when and where? Will they still be friends, or has the war changed them completely?

- What does it cost Annemarie to wear the Star of David necklace? Do any of her friends not want to associate with her because they think she is Jewish?

- Does Uncle Henrik ever get caught smuggling Jews out of the country? How long will the drug on the handkerchief last? Will it get weaker as they continue to use it? Do the Germans ever discover what is happening?

- Are there other neighbors of the Johansens that need help? How many times can they risk taking people to the seashore without arousing suspicion?

- Is the truth about Lise's death ever publicized? If so, are those responsible ever brought to justice?

- Does Annemarie continue to live in Denmark after the war?

Book Report Ideas

There are numerous ways to do a book report. After you have finished reading *Number the Stars,* choose one method of reporting that interests you. It may be an idea that your teacher suggests, an idea of your own, or one of the suggestions below.

- **Create a Billboard**
  Advertise the book *Number the Stars,* using poster board and drawing the wooden frame on with brown markers.

- **Make a "Comic Strip"**
  Show the action of the story by making sketches on long strips of paper using stick figures.

- **Sequence Events**
  Work in a group to list 10 or 15 major events from the book. Write or draw these on index cards, and attach them to a ribbon in sequential order. Hang this from the ceiling for an interesting visual book report!

- **See What I Read?**
  This report is a visual one. A model of a scene from the story can be created, or a likeness of one or more of the characters from the story can be drawn or sculpted.

- **Come to Life!**
  This report is one that lends itself to a group project. A size-appropriate group prepares a scene from the story for dramatization, acts it out, and relates the significance of the scene to the entire book. Costumes and props will add to the dramatization!

- **Guess Who or What!**
  This report takes the form of "Twenty Questions." The reporter gives a series of clues about a character from the story in a vague to precise, general to specific order. After all clues have been given, the identity of the mystery character must be deduced. After the character has been guessed, the same reporter presents another "Twenty Questions" about an event in the story.

- **A Character Comes to Life!**
  Suppose one of the characters in *Number the Stars* came to life and walked into your home or classroom? This report gives a view of what this character sees, hears, and feels as he or she experiences the world in which you live.

- **Sales Talk**
  This report serves as an advertisement to "sell" *Number the Stars* to one or more specific groups. You decide on the group to target and the sales pitch you will use. Include some kind of graphics in your presentation.

- **Coming Attraction!**
  Number the Stars is about to be made into a movie and you have been chosen to design the promotional poster. Include the title and author of the book, a listing of the main characters and the contemporary actors who will play them, a drawing of a scene from the book, and a paragraph synopsis of the story.

- **Literary Interview**
  This report is done in pairs. One student will pretend to be a character in the story, steeped completely in the persona of his or her character. The other student will play the role of a television or radio interviewer, trying to provide the audience with insights into the character's personality and life. It is the responsibility of the partners to create meaningful questions and appropriate responses.

Research Ideas

Describe three things you read in *Number the Stars* that you would like to learn more about.

1. _____

2. _____

3. _____

As you read *Number the Stars,* you encountered many geographical locations, historical events, diverse people, ways of life and religious beliefs that are different from your own. To increase your understanding of the characters and events in the story as well as to recognize more fully Lois Lowry's craft as a writer, research to find out more about these people, places, habits, and things.

Work in groups to research one or more of the areas you named above, or the areas that are mentioned below. Share your findings with the class in any appropriate form of oral presentation.

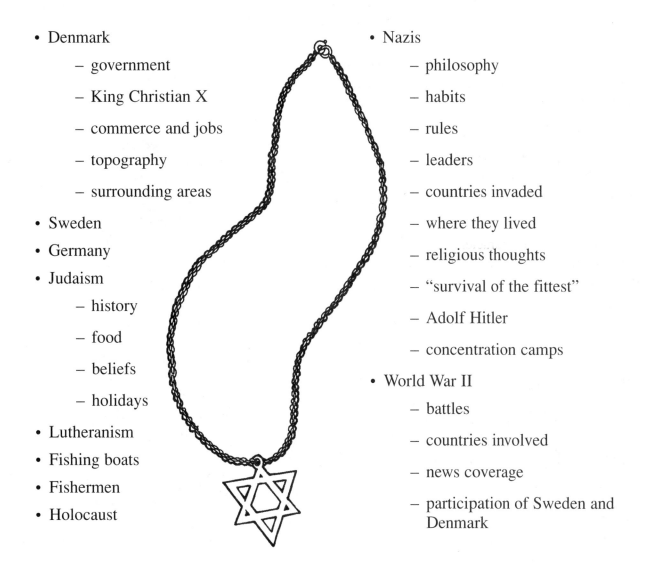

- Denmark
    - government
    - King Christian X
    - commerce and jobs
    - topography
    - surrounding areas
- Sweden
- Germany
- Judaism
    - history
    - food
    - beliefs
    - holidays
- Lutheranism
- Fishing boats
- Fishermen
- Holocaust

- Nazis
    - philosophy
    - habits
    - rules
    - leaders
    - countries invaded
    - where they lived
    - religious thoughts
    - "survival of the fittest"
    - Adolf Hitler
    - concentration camps
- World War II
    - battles
    - countries involved
    - news coverage
    - participation of Sweden and Denmark

A Reunion!

The year is 1950. Annemarie is seventeen years old, and has just graduated from high school. One day, in the mail, she receives a card with familiar-looking handwriting. Opening it up, she discovers that it is a Rosh Hashanah card from Ellen! Ellen is inviting the Johansens to visit them in their new home, and help them begin their new year. In addition to that, an American news reporter finds out about this, and decides that this would make a great human interest story. He/she comes to the reunion and interviews Annemarie and Ellen as they remember their adventure back in 1943.

Pages 40-42 provide directions for having students participate in this reunion, by acting as Annemarie, Ellen, or the news reporter. They may also act as any of the other characters, and adapt the script accordingly.

Getting Ready:

The Jewish New Year is called Rosh Hashanah, or "Head of the Year." It is celebrated on the first two days of the month of Tishi (September-October). It begins the high holy days, ten days of prayer and self-judgment, and is the most solemn period of the Jewish year.

Many Jews have adopted the modern custom of sending a New Year's greeting card to friends and relatives. These carry the traditional greeting, Leshanah Tovah Tikatevu, "May you be inscribed in the Book of Life for a good year."

Make a Shanah Tovah card, and decorate it on the front with something that will reflect the theme of Rosh Hashanah, such as a challah (traditional round or braided bread), a shofar (a ram's horn used to summon Jews to worship), fall fruits, or a scale (the zodiac sign for the month of Tishi, the season when man's fate is weighed).

Inside write, "Leshanah Tovah Tikatevu," and then invite the Johansens to visit.

Prepare traditional Jewish foods to serve at your celebration. Apple slices dipped in honey and honey-flavored cakes, cookies and candies signify a special blessing for a "sweet year." The traditional challah, or bread, is usually baked in a round shape symbolizing the whole new year. Sometimes, however, it is baked in a braid or decorated with a braid on top, symbolizing a ladder which will help prayers rise and "God's blessings descend." You can use frozen bread dough, and braid it after it thaws. Then just let it rise, and bake according to package directions.

The News Reporter Is Here!

Annemarie and Ellen have planned their reunion, and a news reporter from the United States finds out about it. He decides that this will make a great human interest story for a newsreel, newspaper, or radio broadcast back home. Explain to students that most people didn't have televisions back then, but often went to the movies (where they could see a newsreel), listened to the radio, or read the paper. Depending on what media is chosen, set up equipment as follows:

Newsreel: A camcorder works well here. Set up the room to look like a living room (push chairs together and cover with a blanket to look like a couch; put some flowers on a small table, and a picture on the wall). Have the news reporter conduct the interview here. Suggest that students wear 1950's clothing, or that the boys should wear ties, and the girls wear skirts, since the casual attire of today would be unheard of on a newsreel.

Radio: Use a tape recorder to record the interview. The public library usually has records or tapes available of music from the late 1940's and early 1950's. Have the students play a song from the era, interrupt with a news broadcast of the story, and conclude with an advertisement for a typical product of the day. Have students research this, since they may not be aware that video games had not been invented yet! Be sure to have two tape recorders (one for the music and one to record the show) or one tape recorder and one record player, depending on the type of music available.

Newspaper: Have students write up the news article as if it were to be published in the paper. It doesn't need to take the interview format used on the next page, but that can work too. In addition to the article, students should include an advertisement from a product that would have been available at that time. If a computer is available, have them try different fonts for headlines, news, and advertisements. If not, have them try designing fonts by hand (it's harder, but possible).

Interview

Have students work in small groups to conduct interviews in whatever media is chosen from page 41. As a group, they can decide what answer a certain character would have given. During the interview program, the group's members can assume the roles of newscaster, advertiser, character, etc.

Annemarie and Ellen, thank you both for allowing me to be here, and for being willing to tell us your story. Let's begin.

• How did the two of you meet?

_____

_____

• Tell us what life was like before the Germans occupied Denmark.

_____

_____

• How did the Nazis change your life during the time you both lived in Copenhagen?

_____

_____

• Ellen, tell us what happened the day the Jewish Rabbi alerted your family that the Germans were going to relocate the Jews.

_____

_____

• Annemarie, how did your family help the Rosens?

_____

_____

• Ellen, describe your trip to Sweden.

_____

_____

• What message would the two of you like to give the folks who are watching (listening to or reading) this program (paper)?

_____

_____

Unit Test

Matching: Match each of the following items with the phrase that best relates to it.

1. _____ Kirsti   a. cocaine and dried rabbit's blood

2. _____ the "Giraffe"   b. brave, but sloppy

3. _____ "cigarettes"   c. green shoes

4. _____ Resistance   d. code name for Jewish escapees

5. _____ handkerchief   e. Annemarie's best friend

6. _____ Ellen   f. afraid of deep water

7. _____ Mrs. Rosen   g. Danish money

8. _____ Uncle Henrik   h. comparison using "like" or "as"

9. _____ kroner   i. German soldier

10. _____ simile   j. Danish freedom fighters

True or False: Write true or false next to each statement below.

1. _____ Kirsti, Annemarie's older sister, was afraid of the German soldiers.

2. _____ Denmark, Germany, and Sweden were occupied by the Nazis during World War II.

3. _____ The Resistance sank the Danish navy ships.

4. _____ The Rosens were alerted to their danger by the Rabbi.

5. _____ There was no such person as Great-aunt Birte.

Short Answer: Provide a short answer for each of these questions.

1. Annemarie found out that _____and_____ were in the Resistance.

2. _____helped the Jews escape by hiding them in his boat.

3. The man who rode through the streets of Copenhagen with all of Denmark as his guard was _____ .

4. _____owned a button store until the Nazis came.

5. _____was engaged to Lise.

Essay: Write the answers to these questions on the back of this paper.

1. Describe the Rosen family. Include family members, occupation of father, and religion.

2. Why did Mama lie to Annemarie? Was this the right thing to do? Tell why or why not.

3. What happened to Mama on her return from the boat?

Response

Explain the meaning of these quotations from *Number the Stars*.

Note to the teacher: Choose an appropriate number of quotes to which your students should respond.

Chapter 1:   *"Halte!... Why are you running?"*

Chapter 2:   *Each morning, he had come from the palace on his horse, Jubilee, and ridden also through the streets of Copenhagen, greeting his people.*

Chapter 2:   *Redheaded Peter, her sister's fiancé, had not married anyone in the years since Lise's death.*

Chapter 3:   *There were no pink-frosted cupcakes: there hadn't been for months.*

Chapter 3:   *"Well," Annemarie said slowly, "now I think that all of Denmark must be bodyguard for the Jews, as well."*

Chapter 4:   *"Girls," she said, "we have a nice surprise. Tonight Ellen will be coming to stay overnight and to be our guest for a few days! It isn't often we have a visitor."*

Chapter 5:   *Annemarie knew instantly which photographs he had chosen.*

Chapter 6:   *"I'm sending Inge to you today with the children, and she will be bringing you a carton of cigarettes."*

Chapter 8:   *"There has been a death, and tonight your Great-aunt Birte will be resting in the living room, in her casket, before she is buried tomorrow."*

Chapter 9:   *"...it is much easier to be brave if you do not know everything."*

Chapter 10:   *The Lord is rebuilding Jerusalem;*
He gathers in the scattered sons of Israel.
It is He who heals the broken in spirit
and binds up their wounds,
He who numbers the stars one by one...

Chapter 11:   *He inserted the dropper of the bottle into the baby's tiny mouth, and squeezed a few drops of liquid onto her tongue.*

Chapter 11:   *It was an odd word; pride.*

Chapter 12:   *Where was Mama?*

Chapter 13:   *"Mr. Rosen tripped on the step, remember? It must have fallen from his pocket."*

Chapter 13:   *"If any soldiers see you, if they stop you, you must pretend to be nothing more than a little girl. A silly, empty-headed little girl, taking lunch to a fisherman..."*

Chapter 16:   *"Many of the fishermen have built hidden places in their boats. I have, too."*

Chapter 16:   *"Now, thanks to Peter, we will each have such a handkerchief, each boat captain."*

Chapter 17:   *"It is what friends do," Mama had said.*

Conversations

Work in size-appropriate groups to write and perform the conversations that might have occurred in each of the following situations.

- Annemarie and Ellen discuss the incident with the German soldiers on their way home from school. (2 people)

- Kirsti tells her parents her version of meeting the soldiers on the way home from school. (3 people)

- The Rosens give Ellen advice on the importance of getting a good education. (3 people)

- Mama and Papa discuss what happened to Lise. (2 people)

- The Hirsches are confronted by the German soldiers, and taken from their home. (4 - 5 people)

- Mrs. Rosen and Mrs. Johansen discuss the disappearance of Mrs. Hirsch. (2 people)

- Kirsti explains to Annemarie and Ellen why she can't possibly wear green shoes. (3 people)

- After the German soldiers leave their apartment, Mama and Papa sit up late at night discussing what they need to do. (2 people)

- Mama, Annemarie, Ellen, and Kirsti are on the train, discussing what they see in the countryside, and where they are going. (4 people)

- Two or more German soldiers are discussing the disappearance of the Rosens. (2 - 6 people)

- A neighbor of Uncle Henrik stops Annemarie and Ellen on the street, and begins to question them about why they are visiting, and what they are doing. (3 people)

- Peter and Uncle Henrik are discussing the fact that Mama is bringing Ellen to them. (2 people)

- Mama and the girls are getting ready for the funeral. Uncle Henrik arrives and they tell him about it. (5 people)

- Mr. and Mrs. Rosen are traveling to Uncle Henrik's house, and wondering about Ellen and their future. (2 people)

- Uncle Henrik returns to the house to find Mama in a cast. They discuss the events of the day. (2 people)

- The German soldiers know that Jews are escaping from Denmark, but don't know how. Discuss their plans for finding out. (2 or more people)

- The war is over, and King Christian X is discussing with his cabinet what has happened to his country, and how they can rebuild it. (2 or more people)

- Annemarie and Ellen meet many years later, and Annemarie returns the Star of David. They discuss their past and future. (2 people)

Bibliography

Abells, Chana Byers. *The Children We Remember*. (Greenwillow Books, 1986)

Adler, David A. *The Number On My Grandfather's Arm*. (UAHC Press, 1987)

Auerbacher, Inge. *I Am A Star, Child of the Holocaust*. (Simon & Schuster, 1986)

Black, Wallace B. and Blashfield, Jean F. *Blitzkrieg* (Maxwell Macmillan International Publishing Group, 1991)

Benchley, Nathaniel. *Bright Candles: A Novel of the Danish Resistance*. (Harper & Row, 1974)

Butterworth, Emma Macalik. *As the Waltz Was Ending*. (Four Winds Press, 1982)

Dolan, Edward F. *Victory in Europe, The Fall of Hitler's Germany*. (Franklin Watts, 1988)

James, Alan. *Let's Visit Denmark*. (Burke Publishing, 1984)

Knopf, Mildred O. *Around the World Cookbook for Young People*. (Random House, 1966)

Lowry, Lois. *Autumn Street*. (Houghton Mifflin, 1980)

_____ *A Summer to Die*. 1977

_____ *Find a Stranger, Say Goodbye*. 1978

_____ *Anastasia Krupnik*. 1979

_____ *Anastasia Again!* 1981

_____ *Taking Care of Terrific*. 1983

_____ *Anastasia, Ask Your Analyst*. 1984

_____ *The One Hundredth Thing About Caroline*. 1985

_____ *Anastasia and Her Chosen Career*. 1987

_____ *All About Sam*. 1990

Meltzer, Milton. *RESCUE: The Story of How the Gentiles Saved Jews in the Holocaust*. (Harper & Row, 1988)

Messenger, Charles. *The Second World War*. (Franklin Watts, 1989)

Oo Jong, Meindert. *The House of Sixty Fathers*. (Miller Brody Productions, 1974)

Paton Walsh, Jill. *Fireweed*. (Farrar, Straus & Giroux, 1970)

Reiss, Johanna. *The Upstairs Room*. (Thomas Y. Crowell Company, 1972)

Seigal, Aranka. *Upon the Head of the Goat*. (Farrar, Straus & Giroux, 1981)

Sommerfelt, Aimee. *Miriam*. (Criterion Books, 1963)

Stadtler, Bea. *The Holocaust*. (Berhman House, Inc., 1974)

Tames, Richard. *Lifetime – Anne Frank* (Franklin Watts, 1989)

Taylor, Theodore. *The Cay*. (Doubleday & Company, 1969)

Taylor, Theodore. *The Children's War*. (Doubleday & Company, 1971)

Wyman, David S. *The Abandonment of the Jews: America and the Holocaust*. (Pantheon Books, 1984)

Answer Key

Page 10
1. Accept appropriate responses.
2. They are stopped by German soldiers and questioned. The older girls are frightened, but Kirsti is angry.
3. *The Free Dane*s, an illegal newspaper, is brought by Peter Neilson to inform Danish citizens of the work of the Resistance.
4. They are the Danish freedom fighters who sabotaged the Nazis.
5. Lise is Annemarie's older sister who died earlier. She had been engaged to Peter Neilson.
6. Accept all well supported answers.
7. The Rosens are Jewish; Nazis were persecuting them.
8. Kirsti's shoes are made of green fish skin. They dye them black with Mr. Rosen's ink.
9. Ellen spends the night because her parents have been told that they are about to be relocated and need to escape.
10. Order of events: 3, 5, 1, 6, 2, 4.

Page 11
Accept all well-supported answers.

Page 12
Student responses might look like this:

Setting - Copenhagen, Denmark; 1943 (World War II)

Theme - survival of Jews (Accept other well-supported answers)

Protagonist - Annemarie and Ellen

Antagonist - Nazis

Plot - Two friends, one Jewish and one Protestant, must deal with the occupation of their country by the Nazis.

Point of View - 3rd person, limited.

Page 13
Denmark—Yes
Sweden—No
Norway—Yes
Finland—Yes
Poland—Yes
Germany—Yes

Page 15
1. The soldiers burst in and demand to know where the Rosens are.
2. Ellen has dark hair, while the other girls have blonde hair.
3. Papa shows them baby pictures of his three girls, and Lise had dark hair as a baby.
4. The soldiers are gruff and angry; they crush the pictures into the floor.
5. It means a Jew who needs to escape from Denmark.
6. She is afraid that Kirsti will tell the German soldiers that this is Ellen's New Year.
7. Look for the following ideas: red-roofed farm house, very old, crooked, close to the sea, apple tree, bird's nest, meadow, surrounded by woods.
8. Ellen's mother is afraid of the ocean.
9. He says that she died.
10. Accept all reasonable answers.

Page 20
1. Mama lies to protect Annemarie from knowing too much, in case they are confronted by the soldiers.
2. Her parents are there. She is overwhelmed and happy.
3. Mama tells the soldiers that her aunt had died from typhus.
4. The Psalm is a metaphor for God's promise to protect the Jews.
5. The casket contains clothes and blankets.
6. Peter gives the baby a drug to make it sleep. They can't take a chance that it will cry and give away their escape.
7. Peter tells Mr. Rosen to be sure that Uncle Henrik gets the packet.
8. Peter will take half of them through the woods to the boat; Mama will follow with the other half in 20 minutes.
9. Mama is supposed to be gone for one hour; she is gone an hour and a half when Annemarie finds her.
10. Accept all reasonable answers.

Answer Key *(cont.)*

Page 26

1. She trips on a root, falls, and breaks her ankle.

2. Annemarie finds the packet Peter gave Mr. Rosen to take to Henrik.

3. Mama tells Annemarie to put the item in a basket with a lunch for Henrik and to run to get it to the boat as quickly as possible.

4. Annemarie thinks about Little Red Riding Hood.

5. The characters are Red Riding Hood, the grandmother, and the wolf.

6. Red Riding Hood is a picture of Annemarie; the wolf represents the soldiers and their dogs; grandmother is Uncle Henrik.

7. Mama says to act like a silly, empty-headed little girl, taking lunch to a forgetful uncle.

8. Accept all well-supported answers.

9. He finds a handkerchief.

10. Accept all reasonable answers.

Page 29

1. 4,256,240

2. 55,280

3. a little over 1%

4. The percentages are: 46% from Germany, 33% from Sweden, 14% from Norway, 7% from U.S.

5. 4,122,500

6. 1,903,200; 27% were farmers

Page 32

1. Annemarie has to try to milk Blossom.

2. To Uncle Henrik, bravery means that you don't think about how afraid you are; you only think about what has to be done.

3. Annemarie does not feel that she was brave because she feels so frightened.

4. Uncle Henrik smuggles them in a secret hold underneath the deck of his boat.

5. Annemarie learns that Peter is in the Resistance.

6. The handkerchief contains cocaine and dried rabbit's blood. The blood attracts the dogs and the cocaine numbs their sense of smell.

7. The city is jubilant; flags are flown, and church bells are rung.

8. Annemarie learns that Lise had also been part of the Resistance, and had been run down by the Germans when she was fleeing a secret meeting.

9. Annemarie had hidden it in one of Lise's dresses. She will wear it until she can give it to Ellen.

10. The characters were fictitious, but based on real people. The rest were actual happenings in the years 1940 - 1945.

Page 43

Matching:

l. c, 2. i, 3. d, 4. j, 5. a, 6. e, 7. f, 8. b, 9. g, 10. h

True or False:

1. False

2. False

3. True

4. True

5. True

Short Answer:

1. Peter, Lise

2. Uncle Henrik

3. King Christian X

4. Mrs.Hirsch

5. Peter

Essays:

1. Papa was a teacher; Mama was a housewife, and Ellen was a ten-year-old school girl. They were Jewish.

2. Mama lied to Annemarie to protect her, in case Annemarie was ever questioned by the soldiers. Accept either opinion, if it is well-supported.

3. She fell and broke her ankle.

Page 44

Accept all reasonable and well-supported answers.

Page 45

Perform the conversations in class. Ask students to respond to the conversations in several different ways, such as, "Are the conversations realistic?" or, "Are the words the characters say in keeping with their personalities?"